Volume 72 of the Yale Series of Younger Poets

BEGINNING WITH O

Olga Broumas

Foreword by Stanley Kunitz

New Haven and London
Yale University Press

Originally published with assistance from
The Mary Cady Tew Memorial Fund.

Designed by Sally Sullivan.
Set in Monotype Dante by Michael & Winifred Bixler,
Somerville, Massachusetts.
Printed in the United States of America by
The Alpine Press, South Braintree, Mass.

Published in Great Britain, Europe, Africa, and
Asia (except Japan) by Yale University Press, Ltd., London.
Distributed in Australia and New Zealand by
Book & Film Services, Artarmon, N.S.W., Australia; and in
Japan by Harper & Row, Publishers, Tokyo Office.

Library of Congress Cataloging in Publication Data

Broumas, Olga, 1949–
  Beginning with O.

  (Yale series of younger poets; v. 72)
  I. Title. II. Series.
PS3552.R6819B4   811'.5'4   76–49697
ISBN 0–300–02106–2 cloth
ISBN 0–300–02111–9 pbk.

Contents

Acknowledgments

Acknowledgment is made to the following publications for poems that originally appeared in them.

Calyx: "Amazon Twins," "Sleeping Beauty," "Song for Sanna"
Eugene Women's Press: "Thetis"
Journal of the Hellenic Diaspora: "the knife & the bread"
No More Packaged Deals (Jackrabbit Women's Press):
    "Innocence"
Northwest Review: "memory piece / for Baby Jane"
The Pacific: "Leda and the Swan," "Maenad"
The Willamette Valley Observer: "Circe"

Foreword

This is a book of letting go, of wild avowals, unabashed
eroticism; at the same time it is a work of integral imagination,
steeped in the light of Greek myth that is part of the poet's
heritage and imbued with an intuitive sense of dramatic con-
flicts and resolutions, high style, and musical form.

In "Blues / for J. C." Olga Broumas writes:

> Letting go, woman, is not as easy as pride
> or commitment
> to civilization would
> have us think.   Loveletters crowding against the will:
>
> The esplanade of your belly, I said, *that*
> *shallow and gleaming spoon.*   You
> said, *Not quite*
> *an epiphany,* our bodies breathing
> like greedy gills, *not quite*
> *an epiphany, but close, close.*   I loved you
>
> then for that
> willful precision, the same
> precision with which you now
> extricate
> cool as a surgeon
> your amphibian heart . . . .

Here as elsewhere I am struck by the directness and natural-
ness of the inflection, the ease of the controls, and the bright
tangibility of the perceptions. This is a poetry that rests on the
intimate authority and rightness of its sensory data—such par-
ticulars as the belly's "shallow and gleaming spoon," or "our
bodies breathing like greedy gills," or "your amphibian heart"
—a poetry of sensations animated by a fierce and committed
intelligence.

Broumas aspires to be an archaeologist of "the speechless zones of the brain," to grope her way back to the language of the ancestral mothers, an alphabet that defies

> decoding, appears
> to consist of vowels, beginning with O, the O-
> mega, horseshoe, the cave of sound.

In this poem Broumas puts into the mouth of the moon-goddess Artemis, protector of women, twin sister of Apollo, words that seem to define her own nature and credo:

> I am a woman
> who understands
> the necessity of an impulse whose goal or origin
> still lie beyond me.

and, a few lines later,

> I am a woman committed to
> a politics
> of transliteration.

When she concludes,

> We must
> find words
> or burn.

we know that she means it. This is not idle feminist palaver. Her book is as much a political document as it is an impassioned lyric outburst.

"Artemis" stands as one of a group of poems, constituting the first section of the volume, that have their source in Greek myth. It does not seem at all presumptuous for Broumas to link herself with the goddesses of the Hellenic age, for she has honest ties of kinship to that age in blood and spirit. Her witnessing to this heritage gives her work, even in its most reckless and indecorous manifestations, a kind of magnitude, an illusion of heroic scale. In "Demeter" she names the modern writers who have pointed the way for her: "Anne. Sylvia. Virginia. Adrienne" (i.e., Sexton, Plath, Woolf, Rich), and we can see how, in the glow of her imagination, she is already converting them into legend. Several poems in the final section pay Sexton the tribute of imitating, though not without significant variation, her adaptations of fairy tales.

Digging for words and images, Broumas repeatedly strikes water, the female element: "Marine eyes, marine odors."

> Everything live
> (tongue, clitoris, lip and lip)
> swells in its moist shell.

Immersed in her own salt element and yet thirsting for it, she recalls how, as a child, she would dive into the superlative calm of the Greek sea, "enter the suck of the parted waters," and "emerge clean caesarean, flinging live rivulets" from her hair. This key metaphor of immersion and rebirth, from her introductory poem, "Sometimes, as a child," illuminates much that follows.

> In rain-
> green Oregon now, approaching thirty, sometimes
>
> the same
> rare concert of light and spine
> resonates in my bones, as glistening
> starfish, lover, your fingers
> beach up.

Because of their explicit sexuality and Sapphic orientation, Broumas's poems may be considered outrageous in some quarters, but I believe they are destined to achieve more than a *succès de scandale*. We shall all be wiser and—who knows?— maybe purer when we can begin to interpret the alphabet of the body that is being decoded here. Consider the final lines of "Calypso":

> We came together
>
> like months
> in a lunar year, measured in nights, dividing
> perfectly into female phases.   Like women anywhere
> living in groups we had synchronous menses.   And had
> no need of a wound, a puncture, to seal our bond.

Reading that passage, one is impressed by the poet's capacity to transmute complex information into the urgent stuff of poetry. It is not the kind of information that one has been led to expect in verse, even from Broumas's peer group. "How new!" one is quick to exclaim. But another thought supervenes, "How ancient is that lore."

As a mere male, I am conditioned to resist much that Broumas has to say about the gender of oppression and its opposite number, personified in the image of the stone Aphrodite,

> The one with the stone cups
> and the stone face, and the grinding
> stone settled
> between her knees . . . .

Now and then I detect a note of stridency in her voice, a hint of doctrinal overkill, and I am tempted to remind her of Yeats's dictum that we make out of our quarrel with others, rhetoric; out of the quarrel with ourselves, poetry. But is the Yeatsian dialectic universally applicable? In these poems the cause is the flame. On the other side of the anger is an irresistible élan, an exultation—even an ecstasy—of the senses:

> we cross the street, kissing
> against the light, singing, *This*
> *is the woman I woke from sleep, the woman that woke*
> *me sleeping.*
>
> > ("Sleeping Beauty")
>
> Manita's Love
>
> opens herself to me, my sharp
> Jester's tongue, my
> cartwheels of pleasure.   The Queen's own pearl
> at my fingertips, and Manita pealing
>
> my Jester's bells on our four
> small steeples, as Sunday dawns
> clear in February, and God claps and claps
> her one hand.
>
> > ("Innocence")

Among the most impressive features of Broumas's supple art is her command of syntax, rhythm, and tone. Her hedonism extends to the use of language itself; she rollicks in "the cave of sound."

Olga Broumas is the seventy-second winner of the Yale Series of Younger Poets and the first to write in English as an adopted tongue. She was born in Greece in 1949, and her only experience of this country, prior to becoming a resident student in 1967, occurred during her tenth and eleventh years, when her father was stationed in Washington, D.C., as a NATO aide. Her love affair with the English language dates from that childhood visit. It is my pleasure to greet her now, in my valedictory choice for the Yale series, as a new American poet.

Stanley Kunitz

Sometimes, as a child

when the Greek sea
was exceptionally calm
the sun not so much a pinnacle
as a perspiration of light, your brow and the sky
meeting on the horizon, sometimes

you'd dive
from the float, the pier, the stone
promontory, through water so startled
it held the shape of your plunge, and there

in the arrested heat of the afternoon
without thought, effortless
as a mantra turning
you'd turn
in the paused wake of your dive, enter
the suck of the parted waters, you'd emerge

clean caesarean, flinging
live rivulets from your hair, your own
breath arrested.   Something immaculate, a chance

crucial junction: time, light, water
had occurred, you could feel your bones
glisten
translucent as spinal fins.
                              In rain-
green Oregon now, approaching thirty, sometimes

the same
rare concert of light and spine
resonates in my bones, as glistening
starfish, lover, your fingers
beach up.

Twelve Aspects of God   ○   *for Sandra*

Leda and her Swan

You have red toenails, chestnut
hair on your calves, oh let
me love you, the fathers
are lingering in the background
nodding assent.

I dream of you
shedding calico from
slow-motion breasts, I dream
of you leaving with
skinny women, I dream you know.

The fathers are nodding like
overdosed lechers, the fathers approve
with authority: Persian emperors, ordering
that the sun shall rise
every dawn, set
each dusk.   I dream.

White bathroom surfaces
rounded basins you
stand among
loosening
hair, arms, my senses.

The fathers are Dresden figurines
vestigial, anecdotal
small sculptures shaped
by the hands of nuns.   Yours

crimson tipped, take no part in that
crude abnegation.   Scarlet
liturgies shake our room, amaryllis blooms
in your upper thighs, water lily
on mine, fervent delta

the bed afloat, sheer
linen billowing
on the wind: Nile, Amazon, Mississippi.

Amazon Twins

I.

You wanted to compare, and there
we were, eyes on each eye, the lower
lids
squinting
suddenly awake

though the light was dim.   Looking away
some time ago, you'd said
> the eyes are live
> animals, domiciled in our head
but more than the head

is crustacean-like.   Marine
eyes, marine
odors.   Everything live
(tongue, clitoris, lip and lip)
swells in its moist shell.   I remember the light

warped round our bodies finally
crustal, striated with sweat.

II.

In the gazebo-like café, you gave
me food from your plate, alert
to my blood-sweet hungers
double edged
in the glare of the sun's
and our own
twin heat.   Yes, there

we were, breasts on each side, Amazons
adolescent at twentynine
privileged
to keep the bulbs and to feel the blade
swell, breath-sharp
on either side.   In that public place

in that public place.

Triple Muse

I.

Three of us sat
in the early summer, our instruments
cared for, our bodies dark

and one stirred the stones on
the earthen platter, till the salt
veins aligned, and she read the cast:

Whatever is past
and has come to an end
cannot be brought back by sorrow

II.

False things
we've made seem true, by charm, by music.   Faked
any trick when it pleased us

and laughed, faked
too when it didn't.   The audience couldn't tell, invoking
us absently, stroking their fragile beards, waiting

for inspiration
served up like dinner, or sex.   Past.   Here
each of us knows, herself, the mineral-bright pith.

III.

It's been said, we are of one mind.
It's been said, she is happy whom
we, of the muses, love.

Spiral Mountain: the cabin
full of our tools: guitar, tapedeck, video
every night

stars we can cast the dice by.   We are
of one mind, tuning
our instruments to ourselves, by our triple light.

Io

One would know nothing.
One would begin by the touch
return to her body
one would forget
even the three
soft cages
where summer lasts.

One would regret nothing.
One would first touch the mouth
then the warm
pulsing places that wait
that wait
and the last song around them
a shred of light.

A crumpled apron, a headcloth, a veil.
One would keep nothing.

By the still mouths of fear
one would listen.   Desire
would spill past each lip
and caution.   That which is light
would remain.

That which is
still would grow fertile.

Thetis

No.   I'm not tired, the tide
is late tonight, go
with your sisters, go
sleep, go play.

             No?   Then come
closer, sit here, look

where we strung the fruit, hammocks of
apples, dates, orange peel.   Look
at the moon
lolling between them, indolent
as a suckled breast.   Do you understand

child, how the moon, the tide
is our own
image?   Inland
the women call themselves *Tidal Pools*
call their water jars *Women*, insert
sponge and seaweed
under each curly, triangular thatch.   Well

there's the salt lip, finally
drawing back.   You must understand
everything that caresses you

will not be like this
moon-bright water, pleasurable, fertile
only with mollusks and fish.   There are still
other fluids, fecund, tail-whipped
with seed.   There are ways
to evade them.   Go
get a strand

of kelp.   Fold it, down in your palm
like a cup, a hood.   Good.
Squat down beside me.
Facing the moon.

Dactyls

The Palm

Her furrowed heart, her brittle life, her mind
dissected by fate.   Are these adjectives permanent?
She frowns
at her open hand.

Line of the Heart

Up the long hill, the earth rut steamed in the strange sun.
We, walking between its labia, loverlike, palm to palm.

Line of the Mind

The branch splits in two: I will eat both the male
and the female fruit.   Gnaw back the fork to its simple crotch.

Life Line

Metropolis: Mother
city.   Whose columns, bulging
vertically like braced thighs, endure
the centuries, and the brittle light.

The Fate

By the left lintel, lavender.   Through the left
lobe, twin cymbals.   Who dares stop hungry
Fate from her salad, her crazy
leveling meal.

Circe

The Charm

> The fire bites, the fire bites.   Bites
> to the little death.   Bites
>
> till she comes to nothing.   Bites
> on her own sweet tongue.   She goes on.   Biting.

The Anticipation

> They tell me a woman waits, motionless
> till she's wooed.   I wait
>
> spiderlike, effortless as they weave
> even my web for me, tying the cord in knots
>
> with their courting hands.   Such power
> over them.   And the spell
>
> their own.   Who could release them?   Who
> would untie the cord
>
> with a cloven hoof?

The Bite

What I wear in the morning pleases
me: green shirt, skirt of wine.   I am wrapped

in myself as the smell of night
wraps round my sleep when I sleep

outside.   By the time
I get to the corner

bar, corner store, corner construction
site, I become divine.   I turn

men into swine.   Leave
them behind me whistling, grunting, wild.

Maenad

Hell has no fury like women's fury.   Scorned
in their life by the living
sons they themselves
have set loose, like a great gasp
through a fleshy nostril.
Hell has no fury.

Hell has no fury like fury of women.   Scorned
by their daughters who claim paternity, wed-
lock, deliverance
from the pulsing apron-strings of the apron
tied round their omphalos, that maternal
and terrible brand.   Hell has no fury.

Hell has no fury like the fury of women.   Scorned
from birth by their mothers who
must deliver the heritage: signs, methods,
artifacts, what-they-remember
intact to them, and who have no time
for sentiment, only warnings.   Hell has no fury.

And hell has no fury like fury of women.   Scorning
themselves in each other's image
they would deny that image
even to god
as she laughs at them, scornfully
through her cloven maw.   Hell has no rage like this

women's rage.

Aphrodite

The one with the stone cups

and the stone face, and the grinding
stone settled
between her knees, the one with stone

in her bosom, with stones
in her kidneys, a heart of pure
stone, the one with the stony lips, the one

with the thighs of marble, with petrified
genitals, the one whose glance
turns to stone

this idol, stones
through her ears, stones round her neck, her
wrists, round her fingers, a stone

in her navel, stones in her shoes, this
woman so like a stone
statue, herself

a stone, stands
in the stone square, midway
between the stone-high steeple, the stone-

round well, a stone
in her stone-still hand, and a stony will
waiting

for what will land, stiff
as a long stone, on the grinding
stone, on

her lap.

Calypso

I've gathered the women like talismans, one
by one.   They first came for tarot card
gossip, mystified
by my hands, by offers
cut with escape.   They came

undone in my studio, sailing long eyes, heavy
with smoke and wet
with the force of dream: a vagina
folding mandala-like
out of herself, in full bloom.   I used them.   I used

the significance
of each card to uphold the dream, soon
they came back with others.   I let the bitch
twitch in my lap.   I listened.   I let the tea steep
till the pot was black.   Soon

there was no need for cards.   We would use
stills from our daily lives, every woman
a constellation of images, every
portrait each other's chart.
We came together

like months
in a lunar year, measured in nights, dividing
perfectly into female phases.   Like women anywhere
living in groups we had synchronous menses.   And had
no need of a wound, a puncture, to seal our bond.

Demeter

I.

Dependence . . . the male
poet said, *that touchstone
of happiness.* Dependence
on what, happiness
for which one of us, child, segment
of skin and cartilage you have
claimed, and I, yes
have allowed you.
                                    Do
close the shutters, the drawers, the cupboard
doors. They remind
me of open graves—will you die before me, my
bundle of flesh?

II.

What does one say to a child?

What does one say to the little fingers, sticky
with libido, reaching
compulsively out of the dark
enclosure to face
the light?
                    All noble resins:
frankincense, amber, tears of a mother grieving
a mortal child.
                    Anne. Sylvia. Virginia.
Adrienne the last, magnificent last.

III.

Let there be light, let there be light.
                              The terror
of newborns, sliding
down on its medical and
convenient glare.
                    Even your sleep in
a darkened room, and the room itself, shuttered
around you, are analogues
of that place you were shocked from: cold
breath, sharp sight.
                    You refuse sleep.
Rage at the night.   All your life
will you cringe from the dark, bake
your skin in the open sun, hate my gut
that betrayed you?   Child,
                              even here,
in his own book, it says
who held the spotlight
as you delivered yourself, screaming
into its gleaming, mechanical eye.

Artemis

Let's not have tea.   White wine
eases the mind along
the slopes
of the faithful body, helps

any memory once engraved
on the twin
chromosome ribbons, emerge, tentative
from the archaeology of an excised past.

I am a woman
who understands
the necessity of an impulse whose goal or origin
still lie beyond me.   I keep the goat

for more
than the pastoral reasons.   I work
in silver the tongue-like forms
that curve round a throat

an arm-pit, the upper
thigh, whose significance stirs in me
like a curviform alphabet
that defies

decoding, appears
to consist of vowels, beginning with O, the O-
mega, horseshoe, the cave of sound.
What tiny fragments

survive, mangled into our language.
I am a woman committed to
a politics
of transliteration, the methodology

of a mind
stunned at the suddenly
possible shifts of meaning—for which
like amnesiacs

in a ward on fire, we must
find words
or burn.

the Knife & the Bread   ○   *for Stephen*

betrothal / the bride's lament

when all this is over we'll find ourselves
in a big room with wooden floors walls & ceilings
a stone hedge outside & the dogs
barking hard at the threshold

even now we are building this room
we make the roof high stud the crossbeams with hooks
we keep two large trunks rough till the end &
use them for posts here & here now
look how they make the room
strong we say & the splintered bark throws its mouths wide in
laughter & anguish we dare not claim

we'll find ourselves in a shrubbed
acrid land
                the rough logs have worn
from the rub & salt water sheathing them year after year
the leather cords have turned dark
stained & pliant & we've found some names
for the laughter of vanished bark
names our skin calls

for we have yielded by now
to the clasping of nights on this island
where we gyrate like landed squid
immigrants left by even this awkward
most rudimentary language we use
to signify thankfulness appreciation & pain

we will be stranded my love
as lone & exiled as we have never dared hope
& this word will be lost to us too: hope
or will be there like dreams of rain
rushing forests spring rivers like dreams of dreams

we'll grow to crave shadow
to dress our fair limbs with dust

any memory of pale pastel sheets
smooth & ironed & turned down to wait the sliding
of thigh against thigh & the pearly residue of it all
will be there only to taunt us & even then
we will not know the best of it

but will lie on the coarse sand still in the waning moons
& believe that the flapping of wavelets
is maybe the old promise
again in the night come to comfort us
song comfort promise believe will be the new
curses we must atone for

though we'll have song my love
we'll hear the scryings of cleft-winged birds
dashed time & over against the rock
& pick our beat from their gasping hearts
pulsing a minor flood on our lips
here & here

                    yes song & faith too
the old bag of needles might be there
listening & her senile cronies calm peace & solace but
who love who could grant absolution from this
raging clarity its relentless fear &
even if would you want to

gentle rags garnered weeds bitter ashes the days
still pass
            we forget the hammer the cold slate shakes
in morning light we repeat the grief
break the milk's skin
sink what sorrow persists in its creamy torpor
call it dream gone

outside the garden throws hasty vines down the gravel path
& the structure
a half-built & peak-roofed cell
wears the dew's sparkling mail like a sneer

we rise together our bodies blind in venetian light
fat like the birds in our fish-tank windows
& smooth where the sweat still lasts
                                or semen
smooth with the loose pride of now when it's all
over love pride will be first to go
& we stretch our limbs from some odd stiffness
pull on our downy sheaths

when the latch slips its lock this time
past our linked fingers
more doors than this
one are closing

        o

        o

plunging into the improbable

we are partners in this bee
partners
& spell each other against the wall of fame

you will know what i mean, words
are supposed to claw you with
beauty, tear at you
spirant by sonorant
tongue by tongue

some weird mutation of orgasm
a spasm

        o

the film develops in its aluminum skull
life goes on with its glee
love its passion
equally

you or i
trade off words, partners
suddenly & at random: like
lights in the high-rise windows, a flick
of a tongue now
a hiss

        o

we had signed with the brush of thighs
held back all clappers
but one, & that
one pealing
odors of covered sprouts
yeast & shellfish, odors of fluid, the dark-
room dark & the metal bone

what night could wish for more equal meal?

more suitable silver?

　　o

others stalk lovers, the wild
fuck

in this room
the slice of skin that reveals me
to you
is as meaningful, later
sleep carves our body out of a log
we wake up falling

the stage dismantled, pedestal gone
the audience even
dancing to instrumentals

a wooden ladle
twists in our mouth for the alphabet
but the tongue is no soup bone
the teeth give no broth

　　o

the film has developed
prolific in chemical baths: breasts
curving sharply to wrinkled mounds
the glans like an unshelled cervix
the cunt-folds sweating
the ass-hole sweet

here we are, a curve
on a piece of paper, a line of ink
the improbable in high contrast, a contact
sheet, black & white

here we are, fixed
in eidetic memory, film
of the greedy mind, tapedecks & journals, each
other's voice in deep sleep played
back every morning

flesh-toned
the celluloid unfurls
round the cogs with a whisper, the stars
are silent, the sky
exposed

     o

     o

Love Lines

for those islands in the Aegean
whose harbors are too small
for commercial lines

our muffled phone & the through-
town train, tonight i
fuse them
in sleep as their rumble
fades, rhythmically, & another's
sound echoes, a ship's

stack, hooting
desultorily past
small hulled islands, each port a knothole
lapped shut

○

the water is tender, green, curls
softly innocent, a lazy noose in the sunlight
i loved you, i know

now, water swells
wood, lungs, i loved you, i go

past shallows to
sashaying algae to
prowling kelp, remote
inaccessible

as the harbor, no phone
or faith

○

love orbits
us, all night
long, your cock is an instrument
in my palm to gauge by, at breakfast you pour

the coffee, i hold
my tongue, what i keep from you
keeps
me from you, the ship

is fading, like sunlit frost, silver
gleams on our table, mugs shine
red as cranberries, blue as frostbite, i want

to hold
on, not back, brave
morning's fierce tangibility—
tell you

o

still, by the dry light, i grow
edgy, bristle
defenses, a pine-
cone in fire

if i were a man, or you a woman, anything
would be easier than this: one man
you, me
one woman, lost
in the shrinking summer

our breakfast done

o

o

memory piece | for Baby Jane

your touch is gentle on
your own skin, your shoulders love you
at night

your mother calls from across the country
collect, awake
from a bad dream, you are
too far away, she tells you
secrets, your free

hand gathers you
up, knee to nipple, your own
body

becomes your mother
your own lap

    o

you spelled your name like a cabaret
B. J., five feet two inches of
tough luck, you made it

sound good, —baby
three years of balancing
on a madman's pole, with
his tray, his apron
for food & tips
three years

more for tuition, six months
for love

o

in the bathtub you
bathe yourself, with such care
your ex-husband shivers, your breasts

shine on the water
adrift with hair

you've noticed the cat
doesn't leap to your lap in the morning, she
haunts the closets, a neutered
animal, fat
on food

you think of ends, lumescent
periods, islands
at line's term

abortion

you pull the plug & rub
creamrinse on pubic hair still
light with summer

you rinse down spirals
on crescent thighs

o

turning in
to herself, your body finds nothing
hard, nothing quiet, that wish
is blood, you have no wound

that would heal, you are a woman
you bleed

neither pregnant nor fallow, not
pill-controlled, you throw
mud into pots that might
hold water, the same

palm curves on
the wheel that curves round
your belly, at night
i remember, you'd
sing

to yourself

o

o

the knife & the bread

for the women of Cyprus, '74

in the morning
the room is sharp with mirrors
the light is helpless

i skirt
your livewire laughter
i embrace the wall, fat curtains bellying
in on the wind: cooler weather

i tell you violence
perseveres, the light being cruel
itself
to the beveled edges
i look, i cannot forget
though i flap my mind like a breathless tongue

o

i am sick with knives, knives
slashing breasts away, hand-held
knives cutting wounds to be raped
by cocks, thick blunt knives
sheathing blood, knives
paring cheeks away
knives
in the belly

38

apples won't comfort me
this isn't love

this dance i pant from not safe
or ancient, its steps
marred with the fall of women
falling
from cliffs, walls, anything
to escape this war
without national

boundary, this fear
beyond tribes

o

you, over there, dark
as a church, insular
can ignore the light
in the cruel mirrors

you laugh/ a knife
in your
belly would
slice only guts

o

when the enemy comes
the men run to the mountains

they are rebels
they sing to their knives
wash out their hair & prepare themselves
for a manly death

young women hide in the cellars

old women wait

when the enemy comes
they make the old women dance
make them sing/ underground
an infant begins to wail
in her single knowledge

the old ones sing louder
dance faster, fit these new words
to their frenzied song: *daughter, oh*
      throttle her
      or slaughter her
      or gag her on your breast

you have seen their breasts
rolling in mounds, little pyramids
in the soldiers' wake

        o

i slice the bread
in the kitchen, i hold the knife

steady against the grain
that feeds us
all
indiscriminate
as an act of god

i hold the knife
& i slice the bread/ the west
light low on the blade
liquid, exhausted
the food

chaste on the table & powerless
to contain us, how long
can i keep the knife

in its place

    o

    o

Innocence ○ *for Claire, my mother*

Innocence

. . . the sound of one hand clapping

I.

Manita's the Queen.   Love and Love
lying by her, one
on each side.   I
am the Jester, the
smallest one, I roll
round the bed at Manita's feet, the floor
tangled with cast-off garments.   I flick my sharp
tongue at Love.   I adore
Manita
the Queen
at the foot of the bed, each hand so deep
in Loves' collapsible caves.   Manita kneeling
in the midst of Love.
Manita talking
with God.

II.

Manita talking with God.   God
appears

among us, elusive, the extra
hand none of us—Love, Love, Jester, Queen—
can quite locate, fix, or escape.   Extra
hand, extra
pleasure.   A hand

with the glide of a tongue, a hand
precise as an eyelid, a hand with a sense
of smell, a hand that will dance
to its liquid moan.
God's hand

loose on the four of us like a wind
on the grassy hills of the South.

    III.

I take my Love to Manita.   Swift-boned, green-
eyed, dressed in her dark skin and hair, I take my Love in
on fire.   Manita moans.
Manita's hands

flow
delicate as insects, agile
as fish, cool as the shifting water, the night-
quiet lake.   I take my Love to her hands on
fire.   She takes my Love.

    IV.

She takes my Love to her passions, sweet
bruises on her dark skin, her nipples
sucked up like pears, the small
hand of God
inventing
itself again, wind
on Manita's hair.   Neither

Love moves.   Queen and the Jester the
merging shadows on wall and ceiling, the candle thick
as a young tree, bright
with green fire.
Manita's Love

opens herself to me, my sharp
Jester's tongue, my
cartwheels of pleasure.   The Queen's own pearl
at my fingertips, and Manita pealing

my Jester's bells on our four
small steeples, as Sunday dawns
clear in February, and God claps and claps
her one hand.

Four Beginnings / for Kyra

1. You raise
   your face from mine, parting
   my breath like water, hair falling
   away in its own wind, and your eyes—
   green in the light like honey—surfacing
   on my body, awed
   with desire, speechless, this common dream.

2. You bore your marriage like a misconceived
   animal, and have the scars, the pale
   ridged tissue round front and back
   for proof.   For proof.   Tonight

   we cross into each other's language.   I take your hand
   hesitant still with regret
   into that milky landscape, where braille
   is a tongue for lovers, where tongue,
   fingers, lips
   share a lidless eye.

3. I was surprised myself—the image of the lithe
   hermaphroditic lover a staple of
   every fantasy, bought, borrowed, or mine.   We never did
   mention the word, unqualified: I love:
   your hair, I love: your feet, toes, tender nibbles, I love:

I love.   You are the memory
of each desire that ran, dead-end, into a mind
programmed to misconstrue it.   A mind inventing
neurosis, anxiety, phobia, a mind expertly camouflaged
from the thought of love
for a woman, its native
love.

4. I in my narrow body, spellbound
   against your flesh.

Song / for Sanna

. . . in this way the future enters
into us, in order to transform itself
in us before it happens.
                    R. M. Rilke

What hasn't happened
intrudes, so much
hasn't yet happened.   In the steamy

kitchens we meet in, kettles
are always boiling, water for tea, the steep
infusions we occupy
hands and mouth with, steam
filming our breath, a convenient

subterfuge, a disguise
for the now
sharp intake, the measured
outlet of air, the sigh, the gutting
loneliness

of the present where
what hasn't happened will
not be ignored, intrudes, separates
from the conversation like milk
from cream, desire

rising between the cups, brimming
over our saucers, clouding the minty
air, its own
aroma a pungent
stress, once again, you will get
up, put on your coat, go

home to the safer passions, moisture
clinging still to your spoon, as the afternoon
wears on, and I miss, I
miss you.

Lullaby

I see you, centered
along the long
axis of the house, as I come in

to your wide perspective
that endless corridor, the light
drawling forever on the lip of darkness, your long
skin radiant, its stubborn resistance
to summer tan.   I see you

signaling like a white flag
in the square of your mother's crocheted
and labyrinth quilt.   Brown,

black, amber, white, and that treacherous
red like a border around
the luminous hull
of your body.   You leaned

into me like a ship embracing
the waters it was meant to shun, the dangerous
undertow it was meant to float on
and not claim.   My love

this love has not been
forbidden.   Its one risk: sailing
down through the warm laterals of the heart
to a windless bay.   One of our mothers prays for this song

to survive
her own deafened ears, the other
pieces together a second quilt, one that will
cover us, not for shame, nor
decency, but

as the chill
streetlights fluoresce on our light sleep, finally
tucking us in, for warmth.

Blues / for J.C.

Letting go, woman, is not as easy as pride
or commitment
to civilization would
have us think.   Loveletters crowding against the will:

The esplanade of your belly, I said, *that*
shallow and gleaming spoon.   You
said, *Not quite*
an epiphany, our bodies breathing
like greedy gills, *not quite*
an epiphany, but close, close.   I loved you

then for that
willful precision, the same
precision with which you now
extricate
cool as a surgeon
your amphibian heart.   My mouth,

blind in the night to pride, circles
your absence, absurd as one
fish, kissing
compulsively through the vertigo
of the deep

silence
an ocean, dimly perceived
like an aftertaste: my own salt, my fish-
bowl gyrations, my beached
up mouth.

Bitterness

She who loves roses must be patient
and not cry out when she is pierced by thorns.
Sappho

In parody
of a grade B film, our private
self-conscious soapie, as we fall
into the common, suspended disbelief of love, you ask
will I still be
here tomorrow, next week, tonight you ask am I really
here.   My passion delights

and surprises you, comfortable
as you've been without it.   Lulled
comfortable as a float myself in your real
and rounded arms, I can only smile
back, indulgently
at such questions.   In the second reel—

a season of weeks, two
flights across the glamorous Atlantic, one
orgy and the predictable divorce
scenes later—I'm fading out
in the final close-up
alone.   As one

heroine of this
two-bit production to the other, how long
did you, did we both know
the script
meant you to wake up doubting
in those first nights, not me, my daytime
serial solvency, but yours.

Beauty and the Beast

For years I fantasized pain
driving, driving
me over each threshold
I thought I had, till finally
the joy in my flesh would break
loose with the terrible
strain, and undulate
in great spasmic circles, centered
in cunt and heart.   I clung to pain

because, as a drunk
and desperate boy once said, stumbling from the party
into the kitchen and the two
women there, "Pain
is the only reality."   I rolled
on the linoleum with mirth, too close
to his desperation to understand, much less
to help.   Years

of that reality.   Pain the link
to existence: pinch your own tissue, howl
yourself from sleep.   But that night was too soon

after passion
had shocked the marrow alive in my hungry bones.   The boy
fled from my laughter
painfully, and I
leaned and touched, leaned
and touched you, mesmerized, woman, stunned

by the tangible
pleasure that gripped my ribs, every time
like a caged beast, bewildered
by this late, this essential heat.

Cinderella

. . . the joy that isn't shared
I heard, dies young.
Anne Sexton, 1928–1974

Apart from my sisters, estranged
from my mother, I am a woman alone
in a house of men
who secretly
call themselves princes, alone
with me usually, under cover of dark.   I am the one allowed in

to the royal chambers, whose small foot conveniently
fills the slipper of glass.   The woman writer, the lady
umpire, the madam chairman, anyone's wife.
I know what I know.
And I once was glad

of the chance to use it, even alone
in a strange castle, doing overtime on my own, cracking
the royal code.   The princes spoke
in their fathers' language, were eager to praise me
my nimble tongue.   I am a woman in a state of siege, alone

as one piece of laundry, strung on a windy clothesline a
mile long. A woman co-opted by promises: the lure
of a job, the ruse of a choice, a woman forced
to bear witness, falsely
against my kind, as each
other sister was judged inadequate, bitchy, incompetent,
jealous, too thin, too fat.   I know what I know.
What sweet bread I make

57

for myself in this prosperous house
is dirty, what good soup I boil turns
in my mouth to mud.   Give
me my ashes.   A cold stove, a cinder-block pillow, wet
canvas shoes in my sisters', my sisters' hut.   Or I swear

I'll die young
like those favored before me, hand-picked each one
for her joyful heart.

Rapunzel

A woman
who loves a woman
is forever young.
                Anne Sexton

Climb
through my hair, climb in
to me, love

hovers here like a mother's wish.
You might have been, though you're not
my mother.   You let loose like hair, like static
her stilled wish, relentless
in me and constant as
tropical growth.   Every hair

on my skin curled up, my spine
an enraptured circuit, a loop of memory, your first
private touch.   How many women
have yearned
for our lush perennial, found

themselves pregnant, and had
to subdue their heat, drown out their appetite
with pickles and harsh weeds.   How many
grew to confuse greed
with hunger, learned to grow thin on the bitter
root, the mandrake, on their sills.   *Old*

bitch, young
darling.   May those who speak them
choke on their words, their hunger freeze
in their veins like lard.
Less innocent

in my public youth
than you, less forbearing, I'll break the hush
of our cloistered garden, our harvest continuous
as a moan, the tilled bed luminous
with the future
yield.   Red

vows like tulips.   Rows
upon rows of kisses from all lips.

Sleeping Beauty

I sleep, I sleep
too long, sheer hours
hound me, out
of bed and into clothes, I wake
still later, breathless, heart
racing, sleep
peeling off like a hairless
glutton, momentarily
slaked.   Cold

water shocks me
back from the dream.   I see
lovebites like fossils: *something*
that did exist

dreamlike, though
dreams have the perfect alibi, no
fingerprints, evidence
that a mirror could float
back in your own face, gleaming
its silver eye.   Lovebites like fossils.   Evidence.
Strewn

round my neck like a ceremonial
necklace, suddenly
snapped apart.

    o

Blood.   Tears.   The vital
salt of our body.   Each
other's mouth.
Dreamlike

the taste of you
sharpens my tongue like a thousand shells,
bitter, metallic.   I know

as I sleep
that my blood runs clear
as salt
in your mouth, my eyes.

o

City-center, mid-
traffic, I
wake to your public kiss.   Your name
is Judith, your kiss a sign

to the shocked pedestrians, gathered
beneath the light that means
stop
in our culture
where red is a warning, and men
threaten each other with final violence: *I will drink
your blood.*   Your kiss
is for them

a sign of betrayal, your red
lips suspect, unspeakable
liberties as
we cross the street, kissing
against the light, singing, *This
is the woman I woke from sleep, the woman that woke
me sleeping.*

o

o

Rumplestiltskin

First night.
Mid-winter.
Frightened
with pleasure as I came.
Into your arms, salt
crusting the aureoles.
Our white breasts.   Tears
and tears.   You
saying
I don't know
if I'm hurting or loving
you.   I
didn't either.
We went on
trusting.   Your will to care
for me intense
as a laser.   Slowly
my body's cellblocks
yielding
beneath its beam.

I have to write of these things.   We were grown
women, well
traveled in our time.

        o

Did anyone
ever encourage you, you ask
me, casual
in afternoon light.   You blaze
fierce with protective anger as I shake
my head, puzzled, remembering, no
no.   You blaze

a beauty you won't claim.   To name
yourself beautiful makes you as vulnerable
as feeling
pleasure and claiming it
makes me.   I call you lovely.   Over

and over, cradling
your ugly memories as they burst
their banks, tears and tears, I call
you lovely.   Your face
will come to trust that judgment, to bask
in its own clarity like sun.   Grown women.   Turning

heliotropes to our own, to our lovers' eyes.

        o

Laughter.   New in my lungs still, awkward
on my face.   Fingernails
growing back
over decades of scar and habit, bottles
of bitter quinine rubbed into them, and chewed
on just the same.   We are not the same.   Two

women, laughing
in the streets, loose-limbed
with other women.   Such things are dangerous.
Nine million

have burned for less.

o

How to describe
what we didn't know
exists: a mutant organ, its function to feel
intensely, to heal by immersion, a fluid
element, crucial
as amnion, sweet milk
in the suckling months.

Approximations.
The words we need are extinct.

Or if not extinct
badly damaged: the proud Columbia
stubbing
her bound up feet on her dammed
up bed.   Helpless with excrement.   Daily

by accident, against
what has become our will through years
of deprivation, we spawn the fluid
that cradles us, grown
as we are, and at a loss
for words.   Against all currents, upstream

we spawn
in each other's blood.

o

Tongues
sleepwalking in caves.   Pink shells.   Sturdy
diggers.   Archaeologists of the right
the speechless zones
of the brain.

Awake, we lie
if we try to use them, to salvage some part
of the loamy dig.   It's like
forgiving each other, you said
borrowing from your childhood priest.
Sister, to wipe clean

with a musty cloth
what is clean already
is not forgiveness, the clumsy housework
of a bachelor god.   We both know, well
in our prime, which is cleaner: the cave-
dwelling womb, or the colonized
midwife:

the tongue.

o

o

Little Red Riding Hood

I grow old, old
without you, Mother, landscape
of my heart.   No child, no daughter between my bones
has moved, and passed
out screaming, dressed in her mantle of blood

as I did
once through your pelvic scaffold, stretching it
like a wishbone, your tenderest skin
strung on its bow and tightened
against the pain.   I slipped out like an arrow, but not before

the midwife
plunged to her wrist and guided
my baffled head to its first mark.   High forceps
might, in that one instant, have accomplished
what you and that good woman failed
in all these years to do: cramp
me between the temples, hobble
my baby feet.   Dressed in my red hood, howling, I went—

evading
the white-clad doctor and his fancy claims: microscope,
stethoscope, scalpel, all
the better to see with, to hear,
and to eat—straight from your hollowed basket
into the midwife's skirts.   I grew up

good at evading, and when you said,
"Stick to the road and forget the flowers, there's
wolves in those bushes, mind
where you got to go, mind
you get there," I
minded.   I kept

to the road, kept
the hood secret, kept what it sheathed more
secret still.   I opened
it only at night, and with other women
who might be walking the same road to their own
grandma's house, each with her basket of gifts, her small hood
safe in the same part.   I minded well.   I have no daughter

to trace that road, back to your lap with my laden
basket of love.   I'm growing
old, old
without you.   Mother, landscape
of my heart, architect of my body, what other gesture
can I conceive

to make with it
that would reach you, alone
in your house and waiting, across this improbable forest
peopled with wolves and our lost, flower-gathering
sisters they feed on.

Snow White

I could never want her (my mother)
until I myself had been wanted.
By a woman.

Sue Silvermarie

Three women
on a marriage bed, two
mothers and two daughters.
All through the war we slept
like this, grand-
mother, mother, daughter.   Each night
between you, you pushed and pulled
me, willing
from warmth to warmth.

Later we fought so
bitterly through the peace
that father blanched in his uniform,
battlelined forehead milky
beneath the khaki brim.

We fought like mad-
women till the house-
hold shuddered, crockery fell, the bed-
clothes heaved in the only passion
they were, those maddening
peacetime years,
to know.

o

A woman
who loves a woman
who loves a woman
who loves a man.

69

                              If the circle
         be unbroken . . .
                                    Three years
into my marriage I woke with this
from an unspeakable dream
about you, fingers
electric, magnetized, repelling
my husband's flesh.   Blond, clean,
miraculous, this alien
instrument I had learned to hone,
to prize, to pride myself on, instrument
for a music I couldn't dance,
cry or lose
anything to.
                      A curious
music, an un-
catalogued rhyme, mother / daughter, we lay
the both of us awake
that night you straddled
two continents and the wet
opulent ocean to visit us, bringing
your gifts.
                      Like two halves
of a two-colored apple—red
with discovery, green with fear—we lay
hugging the wall between us, whitewash
leaving its telltale tracks.
                                    Already
some part of me had begun
the tally, dividing
the married spoils, claiming
your every gift.

      o

Don't curse me, Mother, I couldn't bear
the bath
of your bitter spittle.
                    No salve
no ointment in a doctor's tube, no brew
in a witch's kettle, no lover's mouth, no friend
or god could heal me
if your heart
turned in anathema, grew stone
against me.
              Defenseless
and naked as the day
I slid from you
twin voices keening and the cord
pulsing our common protest, I'm coming back
back to you
woman, flesh
of your woman's flesh, your fairest, most
faithful mirror,
               my love
transversing me like a filament
wired to the noonday sun.

Receive
me, Mother.

     o

     o

Notes

Twelve Aspects of God

The poems in this section are part of a two-media piece that painter Sandra McKee and I worked on during 1975. It consists of a group of twelve oils of preclassical Greek gods, accompanied by twelve poems. The paintings were completed first and each poem grew out of the specific imagery of its painting, as well as the general significance of the myth. We tried, by using local women in contemporary dress as models, and by using contemporary verbal/visual imagery corresponding to the ancient myths, to express the continuity of those myths, and of female power, through the centuries to our own time. Our information on the specifics, significance, origins, and variations of the myths came primarily from Robert Graves's *The Greek Myths* and *The White Goddess*, and Elizabeth Gould Davis's *The First Sex*.

The paintings and poems were exhibited in September 1975 at the Maude Kerns Gallery, Eugene, Oregon, accompanied at the opening by a reading of the poems. In the spring of 1976 Lane Community College made a three-part presentation of the piece on its educational TV channel.

Io A moon god, often assuming the body of a white cow. She is said to have guarded the secrets of an alphabet closely linked to the lunar calendar and its phases. Because of her chosen totem animal, the cow, she has been described as slow-moving, gentle and sensuous.

Thetis God of the sea. She was attended by a college of fifty water nymphs, the Nereids, and, controlling waters and tidal flow, was also believed to have powers over fertility, impregnation, and birth control.

Dactyls   Five gods that sprang from the imprint of Gaea's left hand on a muddy bank, one for each finger. They were closely linked to the earth, their mother, had oracular powers, especially through palmistry, and lived in sacred groves of Oak. They are believed to be the precursors of the Dryads.

Aphrodite   Originally god of midsummer and death-in-life, she annually destroyed the nominal King in an orgiastic ritual, as the Queen Bee destroys the drone: by mating with him and tearing out his sexual organs. In later years, her male priests practiced ecstatic self-castration.

Calypso   A demigod, possessing the power to grant immortality. She lived on an Ionian island, and is said to have been a painter, a weaver, and an accomplished storyteller.

Artemis   Well-known as the Virgin Hunter. Virginity, well into Christian times, signified absence of matrimony, not chastity. Her silver bow was a symbol of the new moon. The goat was sacred to her.

Triple Muse   The Muse was originally one, then split into three, and later nine, as the arts proliferated. Mount Helicon, the spiral mountain, was their home. Hesiod reports that they could make any falsehood believable through the elegance of meter and form.

the Knife & the Bread

memory piece / for Baby Jane   I am indebted to Charles Wright for the word *lumescent*, from his poem "Congenital," in *Hard Freight*.

Innocence

Bitterness   The epigraph appears in the middle of a page of notes on Sappho. I have been unable to locate it in any of her works. It is possible that I wrote it myself, under her influence, or that it might be from some lyric in the *Greek Anthology*, though here again my efforts to locate it have been unfruitful. At the risk of mysticism, I feel the couplet to be hers, regardless of its actual provenance.